WARS THAT CHANGED AMERICAN HISTORY

America in World War I

Richard Worth

WORLD ALMANAC® LIBRARY

Please visit our Web site at: www.garethstevens.com
For a free color catalog describing World Almanac® Library's list of high-quality books
and multimedia programs, call 1-800-848-2928 (USA) or 1-800-387-3178 (Canada).
World Almanac® Library's fax: (414) 332-3567

Library of Congress Catalog-in-Publication Data

Worth, Richard.
  America in World War I / by Richard Worth. — North American ed.
    p. cm. — (Wars that changed American history)
  Includes bibliographical references and index.
  ISBN-10: 0-8368-7292-4 – ISBN-13: 978-0-8368-7292-7 (lib. bdg.)
  ISBN-10: 0-8368-7301-7 – ISBN-13: 978-0-8368-7301-6 (softcover)
  1. World War, 1914-1918—United States—Juvenile literature. I. Title.
II. Title: America in World War One. III. Title: America in World War 1.
IV. Series.
  D570.W67   2007
  940.3'73—dc22   2006011845

First published in 2007 by
World Almanac® Library
A Member of the WRC Media Family of Companies
330 West Olive Street, Suite 100
Milwaukee, WI 53212 USA

A Creative Media Applications, Inc. Production
Writer: Richard Worth
Design and Production: Alan Barnett, Inc.
Editor: Susan Madoff
Copy Editor: Laurie Lieb
Indexer: Nara Wood
World Almanac® Library editorial direction: Mark J. Sachner
World Almanac® Library editor: Leifa Butrick
World Almanac® Library art direction: Tammy West
World Almanac® Library production: Jessica Morris

Pictures credits: The Granger Collection: cover and pages 6, 29, 41; AP Images: pages 5, 10,
12, 13, 15, 17, 18, 20, 23, 28, 40; North Wind Picture Archives: page 9; New York Public
Library, Astor, Lenox and Tilden Foundations: pages 11, 27, 30, 38; The Library of Congress:
pages 24, 26, 32; maps courtesy of Ortelius Design

Printed in the United States of America

1 2 3 4 5 6 7 8 9 10 09 08 07 06

Table of Contents

Cover: African-American soldiers of the 369th Infantry Regiment served in the trenches on the Western Front during World War I. Often underappreciated because of discrimination, the 369th served longer than any other American regiment but was not allowed to march in the war's victory parade in New York City in 1919.

From the time when America declared its independence in the 1700s to the present, every war in which Americans have fought has been a turning point in the nation's history. All of the major wars of American history have been bloody, and all of them have brought tragic loss of life. Some of them have been credited with great results, while others partly or entirely failed to achieve their goals. Some of them were widely supported; others were controversial and exposed deep divisions within the American people. None will ever be forgotten.

The American Revolution created a new type of nation based on the idea that the government should serve the people. As a result of the Mexican-American War, the young country expanded dramatically. Controversy over slavery in the new territory stoked the broader controversy between Northern and Southern states over the slavery issue and powers of state governments versus the federal government. When the slave states seceded, President Abraham Lincoln led the Union into a war against the Confederacy—the Civil War—that reunited a divided nation and ended slavery.

▼ *Wars have shaped the history of the United States of America since the nation was founded in 1776. Conflict in this millennium continues to alter the decisions the government makes and the role the United States plays on the world stage.*

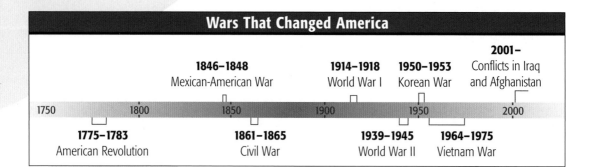

Wars That Changed America

					2001–
		1846–1848		1914–1918	1950–1953	Conflicts in Iraq
		Mexican-American War		World War I	Korean War	and Afghanistan
1750	1800	1850	1900	1950	2000
	1775–1783	1861–1865		1939–1945	1964–1975	
	American Revolution	Civil War		World War II	Vietnam War	

America in World War I

The roles that the United States played in World War I and World War II helped transform the country into a major world power. In both these wars, the entry of the United States helped turn the tide of the war.

Later in the twentieth century, the United States engaged in a Cold War rivalry with the Soviet Union. During this time, the United States fought two wars to prevent the spread of communism. The Korean War essentially ended in a stalemate, and after years of combat in the Vietnam War, the United States withdrew. Both claimed great numbers of American lives, and following its defeat in Vietnam, the United States became more cautious in its use of military force.

That trend changed when the United States led the war that drove invading Iraqi forces from Kuwait in 1990. After the al-Qaeda terrorist attacks of September 11, 2001, the United States again led a war, this time against Afghanistan, which was sheltering al-Qaeda. About two years later, the United States led the invasion that toppled Iraq's dictatorship.

In this book, readers will learn about the United States' reluctant journey toward world power. Once embroiled in the conflicts on the European continent, the United States confirmed its position of global influence.

▲ U.S. Army troops stand in the trenches along the Western Front in France during World War I. The trenches ran from the North Sea to the border of France and Switzerland. They provided shelter for soldiers and cover during battle. Between 1915 and 1917, a series of major battles took place along this front, but the entrenchments, machine guns, and barbed wire protecting the lines kept any significant advances by either side from occurring.

CHAPTER 1

The United States on the World Stage

In 1917, the United States entered World War I. A year later, U.S. forces helped win a victory for the Allies—Great Britain, France, and Belgium. Together they defeated the Central Powers—Germany and Austria-Hungary. Through its participation in World War I, the United States became an important international world power.

Entering onto the World Stage

For the United States, the path to world power had begun many years earlier. During the sixteenth century, Spain had established an empire that stretched from Mexico across most of South America. In the 1820s, that empire crumbled as the Spanish colonies

▼ American industry exploded during World War I because supplies were needed to support the armed forces. With so many men volunteering for the war, women joined the workforce in record numbers.

declared their independence. The United States feared that Spain might regain control of the colonies with the help of other European powers. Therefore, in 1823, President James Monroe issued the **Monroe Doctrine**. It stated that the United States was opposed to any attempt by European nations to establish colonies in the Americas, including North America and South America. Some colonies, however, still existed in Latin America. These included Cuba and Puerto Rico, which were controlled by Spain. With the possession of these colonies, Spain remained a possible threat to the United States.

During the late nineteenth century, the United States expanded the meaning of the Monroe Doctrine. The United States regarded the Western Hemisphere— South America and North America—as an area under its protection. The United States watched political events in Cuba closely. It also investigated the possibility of building a canal through the Isthmus of Panama.

To safeguard the Western Hemisphere, the United States built up its navy. Beginning in the 1880s, Congress spent billions of dollars building naval **cruisers**—large, heavily armored ships made from steel. These ships were designed to protect North American coastlines and assert U.S. power in the Caribbean. During the 1890s, the U.S. navy continued to expand, as large **battleships** were built in navy yards.

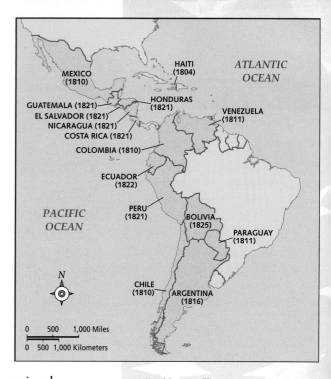

▲ This map illustrates many of Spain's former colonies in North America, South America, and Central America, along with the years they gained their independence.

Hawaii and the Far East

In 1884, Grover Cleveland was elected president of the United States. President Cleveland believed that the vital interests of the United States included not only Latin America but also the Far East. Beginning in 1805, U.S. traders had begun a brisk business with the Hawaiian Islands. Merchants purchased Hawaiian sandalwood and shipped it to China, where it was burned as incense. Interest in Hawaii increased as U.S. planters developed sugar plantations on the islands. In 1876, a special treaty with the U.S. government permitted Hawaiian sugar to be imported into the United States with no taxes. Sugar imports rose from 21 million pounds (9.5 million kilograms) in 1876 to more than 224 million pounds (102 million kg) by 1890.

By this time, Hawaii, still an independent republic, was becoming increasingly controlled by the U.S. government and its commercial interests. The United States also had a military interest in Hawaii. In 1887, the Hawaiian king, Kalakaua, had granted the United States the right to build a naval station at Pearl Harbor. Naval stations in the Pacific Ocean had become increasingly important for U.S. trade. For centuries, ships had been powered by sails. During the nineteenth century, however, ships began using steam engines, which allowed them to move faster. These engines were driven by coal. Merchant ships could not carry enough coal to make trips across the Pacific Ocean. Therefore, coaling stations became essential. These were safe harbors where large ships could take on coal from small coal supply boats instead of trying to refuel in rough seas.

Other European nations were also extending their reach into the Pacific Ocean. Coaling stations were established by Germany and Great Britain in the Samoan Islands. Spain controlled the Philippine Islands, which lay west of Hawaii. In Hawaii, U.S. merchants and planters feared that U.S. interests might be threatened by European colonial powers, such as Spain and Great Britain. These merchants and planters wanted the United States to **annex** Hawaii.

When the U.S. government failed to act, a group of American businessmen formed a secret society called the Hawaiian League. The league was led by Lorrin Thurston, whose grandparents had settled in the Hawaiian Islands. In 1887, the Hawaiian League led an armed revolt against King Kalakaua. The league forced the king to sign the Bayonet Constitution. According to this new constitution, voting in Hawaii was no longer restricted to native Hawaiians. Americans, including the members of the league, could now vote. Most of King Kalakaua's power was transferred to the Hawaiian legislature. Under the new constitution, only large land-owners, like the sugar planters, could be members of the legislature.

Soon afterward, King Kalakaua died. He was succeeded by his sister, Queen Liliuokalani. The queen refused to accept the Bayonet Constitution. She planned to restore the power of the monarch and reclaim Hawaii as an independent nation under Hawaiian rule. The wealthy American merchants and planters refused to see their power reduced. In 1892, Lorrin Thurston sailed to Washington to ask for annexation of the islands. President Benjamin Harrison told him, "You will find an exceedingly sympathetic administration here."

Early in 1893, Queen Liliuokalani prepared to announce a new constitution. Americans, led by Thurston, decided the time had come to act. They asked for support from the U.S. ambassador to Hawaii, John L. Stevens. He provided assistance from an American ship, the USS *Boston*, anchored in the harbor at Honolulu, Hawaii. More than 160

▲ *Queen Liliuokalani, pictured above, was the last reigning monarch of the Hawaiian Islands. She was forced to give up her position in 1893, and in 1898 Hawaii was annexed to the United States.*

armed U.S. troops marched down the main street of Honolulu to demonstrate the power of the United States. This was the only armed force in Honolulu. Queen Liliuokalani was forced to give up her throne. In 1894, Hawaii became an independent republic under the control of a new government, led by wealthy plantation owner Sanford Dole.

Dole and other leading members of the government wanted Hawaii to be annexed by the United States. Although President Harrison was in favor of annexation, his presidency ended in 1893. He was replaced by Grover Cleveland, who opposed annexation. Cleveland did not believe that the United States should begin to acquire colonies. In 1896, a new U.S. president, William McKinley, was elected. By then, the mood in the United States was changing. In 1898, the United States annexed Hawaii. That same year, the United States went to war with Spain.

The Spanish-American War

In 1895, a revolt broke out on the island of Cuba against the colonial government of Spain. The Spanish ruthlessly tried to put down the revolt, executing Cuban rebel leaders and burning peasant villages. Many Americans were outraged at the policies of the Spanish. The Republican administration of President McKinley was sympathetic to the cause of Cuban independence. McKinley also feared that the revolution might be very costly for Spain, forcing Spain to sell the island to another powerful European nation, such as Germany. Out of con-

▼ *Lifeboats rescue surviving crewmen of the* USS Maine *after an underground explosion destroyed the battleship on the evening of February 15, 1898, while it was anchored in the harbor of Havana, Cuba. The destruction of the ship was a catalyst for the outbreak of the Spanish-American War. The United States officially declared war on Spain on April 25, 1898.*

cern that Cuba might provide some European nations with an important presence in the United States' backyard, some members of Congress even favored invading Cuba in order to take the island away from Spain. Nevertheless, McKinley was, at first, opposed to war with Spain as an option. Early in 1898, however, riots erupted in Havana, the capital of Cuba. Many Cubans called for independence. The United States sent the battleship *Maine* to Havana to safeguard U.S. citizens living in Cuba and show support for the Cuban rebels. In February, the *Maine* blew up in Havana harbor. The explosion killed 260 sailors. Many people in the United States believed that the Spanish had blown up the battleship, although there was no conclusive proof showing how the ship had been destroyed. Shortly after the explosion, the *New York Journal* ran a headline that would become a rallying cry for those who favored U.S. military intervention in Cuba— "Remember the *Maine!* To Hell with Spain!" Many members of Congress were already calling for war with Spain. Powerful newspapers, like the *New York Journal*, also urged the president to go to war. In April, the United States finally declared war against Spain.

On April 26, shortly after the declaration of war, Commodore George Dewey, commander of the U.S. Asiatic Squadron, received a message from the U.S. Navy Department. Dewey was ordered to steam toward the Philippines. His mission was simple: "capture or destroy" the Spanish fleet in the Pacific. Dewey's goal was to trap the Spanish Navy in Manila Bay. A successful mission would prevent the fleet from sailing to Cuba. To further the goal of disabling Spain's naval power in the Pacific, the United States planned to take

▲ *U.S. cruisers form a line in Manila Bay, Philippines, to batter Spain's ships with gunfire. Commodore George Dewey's victory over the Spanish prevented the enemy's ships from sailing to Cuba and putting down the rebel forces calling for independence there.*

Theodore Roosevelt

Theodore Roosevelt, pictured above, may have benefited more than any other person who fought in the Spanish-American War. During the war, newspaper correspondents wrote widely about Roosevelt's heroism on San Juan Heights. Soon after the war ended, Roosevelt himself published a book about the conflict, entitled *The Rough Riders*. He returned to his home state of New York, where he was a popular war hero. The Republican Party nominated him for governor, and he was elected in November 1898. Two years later, Republican leaders decided that Roosevelt should run as the vice presidential nominee with President McKinley, who was seeking a second term. McKinley and Roosevelt were overwhelmingly elected in 1900. Less than a year later, President McKinley was assassinated. In September 1901, Theodore Roosevelt, at age forty-two, became the youngest man ever to fill the office of president of the United States.

control of the Philippines from Spain. Dewey's fleet included four large cruisers and two smaller gunboats.

Manila, the capital of the Philippines, was protected by a Spanish fleet under the command of Admiral Patricio Montojo. Under the cover of darkness on the night of April 30, Commodore Dewey approached Manila Bay. As dawn broke, Dewey ordered his ships to approach the Spanish in a single line so each U.S. cruiser could fire its guns as it passed in front of the Spanish ships. At 5:22 A.M., May 1, 1898, Commodore Dewey gave the order to start the naval battle. As a band struck up the U.S. national anthem, "The Star-Spangled Banner," Dewey's ships began firing. Superior U.S. firepower had an immediate and devastating effect on the Spanish cruisers. They were knocked out of action within two hours.

Dewey did not, however, have enough troops to take control of the entire city of Manila. In a message he sent to Washington, D.C., Dewey said, "I control bay completely and can take city at any time, but I have not sufficient men to hold." He awaited reinforcements to follow up his victory at Manila. About two months later, eleven thousand American troops were sent to the Philippines. After a brief battle between U.S. and Spanish forces, Spain surrendered Manila.

While Dewey was in the Philippines, President McKinley was focused on the war in Cuba. In April 1898, McKinley asked for 125,000 volunteers to join the army for a short time to fight in the Spanish-American War. Among the first men to volunteer was Assistant Secretary of the Navy Theodore Roosevelt. He immediately resigned from the Navy Department and became a colonel in a cavalry unit known as the Rough Riders. In June, the Rough Riders, along with other army units, left their camps in Florida and sailed for Cuba.

America in World War I

Once they landed on the south coast of Cuba, the U.S. troops prepared to assault the Spanish soldiers guarding the Cuban city of Santiago. The Spanish defended a position in San Juan Heights, a line of hills outside the city. U.S. troops approaching San Juan Heights were pinned down by Spanish fire. Among them were Colonel Roosevelt and the Rough Riders. As Roosevelt put it, "bullets drove in sheets through the trees and the tall jungle grass, making a peculiar whirring or rustling sound; some of the bullets seemed to pop in the air."

Eventually, Roosevelt received the order for the Rough Riders to advance. Astride his horse, Texas, he led his men up San Juan Heights. Other U.S. Army units also mounted a strong charge. The attack was too much for the Spanish, who eventually retreated. On July 16, 1898, Santiago finally surrendered, and the U.S. Army controlled the entire eastern part of Cuba.

Shortly after the surrender, U.S. forces invaded the nearby Spanish island of Puerto Rico. They easily defeated the Spanish troops holding the island and captured several of the major cities.

During the fall, U.S. and Spanish representatives met in Paris, France, to discuss peace terms. On December 10, 1898, after many disagreements, they signed the Treaty of Paris. Under the terms of the treaty, the United States took control of Cuba, Puerto Rico, and, in the Pacific, the Spanish island colony of Guam and the Philippines. As U.S. Secretary of State John Hay said, the conflict with Spain was "a splendid little war." The Spanish-American War signaled a change in U.S. foreign policy and the role of the United States in other parts of the world. For the first time, the United

▲ *Future president Theodore Roosevelt (center, wearing glasses) led his battalion of soldiers known as the Rough Riders to victory in the battle of San Juan Heights.*

The Panama Canal

- The U.S. cargo ship *Ancon* was the first vessel to pass through the canal on August 15, 1914.

- A boat traveling from New York to San Francisco saves 7,872 miles (12,666 km) by using the canal instead of going around Cape Horn.

- A ship takes eight to ten hours to pass through the canal while being gradually lifted or lowered 85 feet (26 meters).

- The Panama Canal Commission employs about nine thousand U.S. and Panamanian citizens to run the canal.

States became an international power. It now had its own colonies—which it was determined to control.

The Panama Canal

In November 1898, Theodore Roosevelt was elected president. He continued to change U.S. foreign policy. The new president firmly believed that the United States had an important role to play on the international stage. Roosevelt remained president until 1909. During his years in office, the size of the U.S. navy almost doubled—reaching more than sixty large warships. Roosevelt believed that a strong navy was essential to protect U.S. interests in the Pacific Ocean as well as in the Caribbean.

Safeguarding these interests, Roosevelt thought, would be made much easier by the construction of a **canal** across Central America. During the Spanish-American War, the U.S. battleship *Oregon* had required sixty-six days to travel from the Pacific Ocean around the tip of South America to Cuba. A canal through Central America would vastly cut the distance and, therefore, the time of such a voyage.

Roosevelt considered two possible routes for a canal. One route cut across Nicaragua. This route, covering 200 miles (320 kilometers), followed existing river channels that already ran through the country. A much shorter route, only 50 miles (80 km) long, ran across the Isthmus of Panama, where there were no river channels. Panama was controlled by Colombia, a much larger country on its southern border. The Panamanians wanted their independence, and they had revolted repeatedly in the past. Each revolt was put down by the Colombian government.

The Roosevelt administration reached an agreement with the Colombian government for the rights to build a canal across Panama. The United States agreed

America in World War I

to give Colombia $10 million and make an annual payment of $250,000. The Colombian congress, however, refused to accept the agreement. Many Colombians feared that U.S. military power was so strong that the United States would take over Panama. In addition, some Panamanian leaders wanted to hold out for more money. Roosevelt was very angry about the outcome.

Meanwhile, the U.S. government became aware that Panamanians were planning to stage another revolt to achieve independence. In November 1903, the conflict broke out in Panama. President Roosevelt saw an opportunity to obtain the land he needed for a canal. He sent U.S. ships to the Panamanian coast, preventing the Colombian government from shipping in troops to put down the revolt. The Panamanians succeeded in gaining their independence and establishing a new government. Roosevelt immediately sent U.S. representatives to Panama to support the new regime. Panama then agreed to permit the United States to build a canal across the isthmus. The canal was completed in 1914.

The Great White Fleet

During his last two years in office, President Roosevelt sent the U.S. fleet on a peace mission, visiting many ports around the world. The Great White Fleet, so-called because the ships were painted white, included sixteen giant battleships, symbols of U.S. military might. Roosevelt was showing the world that the United States had become an important world power.

The battleships of the fleet were manned by fourteen thousand sailors and covered about 43,000 miles (69,000 km). The fleet put in at twenty ports of call on six continents. The USS *Connecticut* led the way, sailing from Hampton Roads, Virginia, to Trinidad, British West Indies; Rio de Janeiro, Brazil; Sandy Point, Chile; Callao, Peru; Magdalena Bay, Mexico; and up the west coast of North America, arriving in San Francisco in May 1908.

Big Stick Foreign Policy

President Roosevelt's action in Panama was part of a foreign policy he called Big Stick Diplomacy, following a speech containing a phrase for which he would become known: "Speak softly and carry a big stick; you will go far." This meant that he would conduct **negotiations** backed by the threat of force. The president extended the Big Stick policy to other parts of Latin America. In 1904, the president issued the Roosevelt Corollary to the Monroe Doctrine. This document stated that the United States had the right to interfere if any Latin American country was involved in "wrongdoing."

When Roosevelt left the presidency, he was succeeded by Republican William Howard Taft, elected in 1908. Taft had served as Roosevelt's secretary of war. President Taft continued many of the policies followed by Roosevelt, but used a quieter approach. Instead of the Big Stick, President Taft pursued **Dollar Diplomacy**. He encouraged U.S. business leaders to put large sums of money into Latin America. He thought that investing in large farms, mines, and railroads would allow the United States to increase its influence over Latin American affairs. Many Latin American nations, however, resented these investors.

By 1913, the last year of Taft's administration, the United States was unquestionably the most powerful nation in the Western Hemisphere. Leading European and Asian nations also recognized the United States as a major power. As the citizens and government of the United States would soon discover, this change in stature and influence would produce another change—the expectation of increased U.S. involvement in the affairs of nations far from the United States and its Latin American backyard.

America in World War I

CHAPTER 2

The Coming of World War I

I n 1912, Woodrow Wilson, a Democrat, was elected president of the United States. After his election, Wilson continued many of the same policies that Taft and Roosevelt had followed in Latin America. These policies immediately involved the new president in Mexican affairs. Nevertheless, much of Wilson's term in office was focused on World War I, which began raging across Europe in 1914. This conflict presented new challenges and led to an expanded role for the United States as an international world power.

Conflict in Mexico

In the early years of the nineteenth century, Mexican dictator Porfirio Díaz welcomed American investment in Mexico. Americans helped develop Mexican oil wells. Oil enriched those few landowners who controlled the property where the oil was discovered, but most Mexicans remained poor. In 1910, Mexican revolutionaries overthrew Díaz. In his place, Francisco Madero was elected president.

Madero did not have the support of the Mexican army, which overthrew him in 1913. The leader of the army, General Victoriano Huerta, became president of Mexico.

▼ *Pancho Villa leads his rebel army in attacks on U.S. citizens living in Mexico in 1916. Pursued by U.S. forces, Villa eluded capture but was later assassinated by political rivals in Mexico in 1923.*

Pancho Villa

Pancho Villa's real name was Doroteo Arango, pictured above. He was born in 1878 on the **hacienda** of a large landowner where Arango's parents worked and lived. When he was still a teenager, Arango saw his sister attacked by the landowner. Vowing revenge, Arango joined a group of outlaws led by a bandit named Pancho Villa. Arango admired Villa, and after the leader was killed during one of his raids, Arango began calling himself by Villa's name. During the early twentieth century, Villa helped lead the revolt that unseated Porfirio Díaz. Although Villa genuinely wanted to provide the Mexican poor with a better life, he was also a thief who robbed innocent citizens and murdered some of those who tried to stop him.

President Wilson, who strongly believed in the principles of **democracy**, regarded Huerta as a dictator. Like President Roosevelt before him, Wilson decided to use American power to force his will on a Latin American nation. In April 1914, Wilson sent American ships to the Mexican port of Veracruz. He wanted to prevent arms from Europe, which were being shipped to Huerta, from ever reaching Mexico. U.S. soldiers took control of the city, killing 126 Mexicans. Soon afterward, Huerta was overthrown by a rebel army led by Venustiano Carranza and supported by the United States.

President Carranza had barely taken office before he faced a rebellion by some of his own generals. Emiliano Zapata and Francisco "Pancho" Villa believed that Carranza should immediately begin land reform in Mexico. Both Zapata and Villa championed the poor farmers and wanted to see them get some of the land controlled by the rich landowners. When Carranza did not act immediately, Zapata and Villa began a revolt. At first President Wilson backed Villa. Villa's soldiers, however, were rapidly defeated by Carranza's army. President Wilson then gave U.S. support to the Carranza government.

Pancho Villa was upset at losing U.S. support. Therefore, he tried to provoke President Wilson into invading Mexico. In January 1916, Villa stopped a train carrying some Americans in northern Mexico and murdered them. Two months later, Villa and his men entered the U.S. town of Columbus, New Mexico, and killed nineteen Americans before Villa escaped back across the Mexican border. Villa assumed that Wilson would send U.S. troops into Mexico if he believed Carranza could not protect Americans living there. He was correct.

In late March, President Wilson ordered General John J. Pershing to lead American troops into Mexico to stop Villa. General Pershing and his troops were unable to locate Villa and capture him. President Carranza was not willing to stop Villa, he was angry with the United States government because its soldiers were invading his country. U.S. and Mexican troops clashed inside Mexico, and eighteen U.S. soldiers were casualties in the battle. A full-scale war almost broke out between Mexico and the United States. Finally, Wilson withdrew U.S. troops from Mexico. These troops were needed for a much larger conflict raging in Europe—World War I.

Events Leading Up to World War I

World War I grew out of severe tensions that had developed among the major powers of Europe. France and Germany distrusted each other. In 1870, during the Franco-Prussian War, Germany had defeated the French armies and captured territory in eastern France. France hoped that, if another war occurred, it would be victorious and take back this land. France began rebuilding its armies. In addition, the French formed an alliance with Russia and Great Britain. The Russians had a powerful army to defend their huge empire in Eastern Europe and Asia. Although Britain had a small army, it had built the most powerful naval fleet in the world.

Germany also began building up its own fleet to oppose Britain's naval power. During the early twentieth century, a naval

▼ On the eve of World War I, Austria-Hungary was a large nation allied with a powerful Germany. This map shows the nations that made up the Allied powers (including Great Britain, France, and Russia), the Central Powers (Germany, Austria-Hungary, the Ottoman Empire, and Bulgaria), and the countries that remained **neutral** throughout the war.

race was under way between Germany and Great Britain to determine which nation could build the largest fleet. Meanwhile, Germany formed an alliance with another European power, Austria-Hungary. At the same time, conflicts were breaking out in the Austro-Hungarian Empire. The Austro-Hungarian Empire was located in central Europe. It included many different national groups, such as Poles, Serbs, Czechs, Italians, and Hungarians. Some of the ethnic groups, such as the Serbs, wanted independence. The Serbs wanted to join the independent Kingdom of Serbia.

By 1914, Europe was simmering with tension. A single incident might lead to war. That incident occurred when Archduke Franz Ferdinand, heir to the Austro-Hungarian throne, was visiting Sarajevo, a city in the

▼ An artist's rendition shows the assassination of Archduke Franz Ferdinand of Austria-Hungary and his wife, Countess Sophie Chotek, during their visit to Sarajevo, Bosnia, on June 28, 1914. The assassin, Serbian nationalist Gavrilo Princip of the Black Hand, was later captured.

Austro-Hungarian territory of Bosnia. On June 28, 1914, the archduke and his wife Sophie were assassinated by a Bosnian Serb student, Gavrilo Princip, who belonged to a radical group called the Black Hand. The members of the Black Hand wanted Bosnia to become part of the independent Kingdom of Serbia, located near Austria-Hungary.

Although Princip was caught, the incident did not end there. Police investigations revealed that the Black Hand had support inside the government of the Kingdom of Serbia. On July 23, the Austro-Hungarian emperor Franz Joseph demanded that his investigators should be allowed to enter Serbia to investigate the Black Hand radicals. The Serbian government regarded this demand as a violation of its independence. Serbian officials believed that only they should have the authority to investigate a radical group located in their country.

Austria-Hungary knew that its demands would never be accepted by Serbia. Emperor Franz Joseph also realized that war might break out between his empire and the Serbs. Before making the demands, Austro-Hungarian leaders had discussed the situation with their allies in Germany. German emperor William II (also known as Kaiser Wilhelm) had told Austro-Hungarian leaders that he would back them with his armies if war broke out and they needed German support. Meanwhile, Serbia had turned to Russia for support. Russian czar Nicholas II was a strong supporter of the Serbs and promised to back them in case of war with Austria-Hungary.

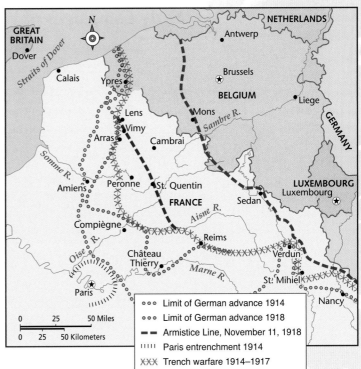

Serbia turned down the Austro-Hungarian demands. On July 28, 1914, Austria-Hungary declared war on Serbia. Russia began to gather its troops to assist Serbia. As a result, Germany came to the defense of Austria-Hungary and declared war on Russia on August 1, 1914. Two days later, Germany also went to war with France. The Germans believed that France might be about to invade their country in order to reclaim territory they had lost in the Franco-Prussian War. German troops poured through Belgium, a neutral country. Soon afterward Great Britain entered the war to support the Belgians and the French. Italy joined the war on the side of the Allies (France and Great Britain).

▲ *The Western Front stretched 475 miles (760 km) from the Swiss border to the North Sea. The line of trenches and dugouts, carved out by soldiers of both armies and protected by barbed wire, was barely altered during the four years of attacks and battles, which bombarded the troops defending their territory on both sides.*

Life in the Trenches

Soldiers along the Western Front lived underground and emerged to fight the enemy in deep ravines called trenches. Soldiers ate and slept underground when they were not manning trenches. They came out from underground, carrying rifles, to occupy these trenches. From these ravines, they poked their heads up and fired at the enemy. Soldiers also strung **barbed wire** in front of the trenches. The barbed wire was designed to prevent enemy troops from entering the trenches in sneak attacks.

Soldiers living in the trenches endured many hardships. The trenches were dug in soil made up of clay or sand and often became flooded during rainstorms. Soldiers standing in the muddy water could develop trench foot, a serious infection of the feet caused by the cold, wet, and dirty conditions. Rats swarmed through the dugouts, and soldiers suffered from lice infestations. During battle, soldiers living in trenches often went without food for days.

Early Campaigns of World War I

The German invasion that began in August 1914 was part of a large **flanking movement** aimed at northern France. Germany's war plans called for its armies to move along the north coast of France. This position would enable them to flank, or surround the French armies that were lying in wait in eastern France, facing Germany. After flanking these armies, German troops planned to strike Paris, located in central France. They expected to capture Paris and assault the French armies from the rear. Meanwhile, another German army would attack the French from the front.

As German troops moved across Belgium, they committed terrible acts of violence. Once the German troops reached French soil, they drove toward Paris. French and British troops stopped the German attack, however, east of Paris at the Marne River. At the Battle of the Marne, the Allies drove the Germans back toward eastern France. Both sides then began to **fortify** a long line of defenses.

French and English forces on one side, and German forces on the other side, dug themselves in under the ground. By living underground, they hoped to protect themselves from being bombarded by heavy **artillery** from the opposing side. Trench lines ran for 475 miles (760 km) from the North Sea off the coast of Belgium to the mountains of Switzerland. Most of the lines ran through France, east of Paris. These lines of trenches were called the **Western Front**.

For the next four years, enemy soldiers on the Western Front fought a series of bloody battles. The French and English tried to drive the Germans out of France and Belgium. The Germans tried to push the Allies back toward Paris. Neither side, however, succeeded in achieving total victory.

CHAPTER 3

The United States Maintains Neutrality

During the early years of World War I, President Wilson refused to take sides in the conflict. Instead, the United States maintained an official policy of neutrality between the Allies and the Central Powers—Germany, Austria-Hungary, the Ottoman Empire, and Bulgaria.

▼ *U.S. marines quickly don their gas masks during an attack near Verdun, France, in 1918.*

23

► *Crowds of people, some in rowboats, gather around a beached German U-boat, while others congregate on the submarine's deck. Battered by bomb damage, the abandoned vessel floated ashore on the south coast of England during the war.*

U.S. Policies toward Europe

Since the founding of the United States, U.S. leaders had believed that they should stay out of the affairs of Europe. For many years, the United States had been far less powerful than nations such as France and Great Britain. Thus, U.S. presidents did not want to risk becoming involved in a European war. In addition, the United States was separated from Europe by the broad Atlantic Ocean. Most Americans believed that this barrier kept them safe from European conflicts.

President Wilson realized that public opinion in the U.S. did not support involvement in the war. Some Americans were German immigrants. They supported Germany. Others supported the Allies. Many Americans felt a strong tie to Great Britain. They spoke the same language, and the United States had originally been settled by English colonists.

President Wilson therefore supported a policy of neutrality. As Wilson put it in August 1914, "Every man who really loves America will act and speak in the true spirit of neutrality, which is the spirit of... fairness and friendliness to all concerned."

Nevertheless, Wilson did not stop private American banks from making loans to the Allies to help them pay for war supplies. In addition, the president allowed U.S. companies to sell these supplies to Great Britain and France.

U.S. ships that took supplies to the Allies ran serious risks. Germany was trying to **blockade** Great Britain and prevent supplies from reaching its shores. The Germans relied on submarines for the blockade. Submarines traveled under water, where they could not be seen, and used **torpedoes**, fired beneath the surface, to sink enemy ships. In 1915, the German government announced that its submarines, called U-boats, would sink any neutral ships that tried to aid Great Britain. President Wilson asked that the Germans stop using this tactic, but the German government did not comply.

German Submarine Warfare

Then, in May 1915, a German U-boat sank the British passenger ship *Lusitania*. Almost twelve hundred people died, including 128 American passengers. Despite British assurances that no war supplies were on the ship, the Germans believed that the *Lusitania* had been bringing ammunition and other goods to the Allies.

President Wilson was outraged. He demanded that the German government stop attacking passenger ships. Germany did not want to anger the United States and possibly increase its support for the Allies. Therefore, the German government agreed to Wilson's demand. In 1916, however, a German submarine torpedoed another British passenger ship. This was the ocean liner *Sussex*, sailing in the English Channel, off the coast of Great Britain. Fifty passengers died, including three Americans. Wilson

Peace Efforts

President Wilson hoped that by remaining neutral, he might bring both sides together for peace talks to end World War I. In 1915, he sent his closest adviser, Colonel Edward House, to Europe. Colonel House held meetings with the Germans, the French, and the English. These meetings, however, did not bring an end to the war. Both sides were unwilling to negotiate, still believing that they could achieve a victory. The Germans believed that they could capture Paris. The Allies believed that they could drive the Germans out of France and Belgium. Late in 1916, President Wilson tried once again to begin a peace conference, but both sides were still convinced that they could wear out their enemies and win the war. Finally, Wilson gave up his attempts to bring both sides together. Instead, he announced his own view of how peace should be achieved. In a speech to Congress, Wilson called for "a peace without victory." In other words, neither side should try to destroy the other and claim victory. Nor should either side try to force the other to pay a huge amount of money for damages caused during the war.

The Plattsburg Movement

Beginning in 1913, Army Chief of Staff General Leonard Wood, pictured above, tried to increase the number of trained American officers. He opened a training program for college students who volunteered to attend military camps during the summer. The program was known as the Plattsburg Movement, named after one of these camps that was located at Plattsburg, New York. The training program expanded during World War I. By 1915, there were four camps that had trained almost four thousand volunteers. By 1916, that number had increased to ten thousand volunteers. Among Americans, support for preparedness was growing. By 1917, when the United States finally entered the war, these trained officers provided important leadership for the army.

once again demanded that the Germans stop attacking unarmed passenger ships. The German government agreed. The Sussex Pledge, issued by the German government on May 4, 1916, stated Germany's intentions. Meanwhile, the United States still maintained a policy of neutrality.

American Preparedness

By 1916, most Americans still believed that the United States should not become involved in World War I. Nevertheless, the sinking of the *Lusitania* turned many people against Germany. Meanwhile, in Europe, the war was a **stalemate**. At Verdun and the Somme, a river in France, giant armies battled each other to a standstill. The casualties were enormous. At the Somme, the Allied powers saw more than 600,000 soldiers killed and wounded. The Germans lost about 500,000 soldiers.

President Wilson still wanted to keep the United States out of the war. He knew that most Americans did not want to go to war. Wilson also realized, however, that the Allies could not defeat Germany. The Allies simply did not have enough manpower to drive the Germans out of France and Belgium. If the Allies were weakened or eventually defeated, German submarines might one day enter U.S. waters and threaten the United States. Therefore, President Wilson developed a policy of preparedness. This meant that the United States should be prepared to defend itself and the Western Hemisphere in the event of an attack on U.S. soil. In 1916, Wilson convinced Congress to increase the size of the U.S. army and navy. The Naval Act of 1916 called for building ten new battleships, sixteen cruisers, and seventy-two submarines. That same year, the National Defense Act enlarged the U.S. army to 175,000 soldiers.

CHAPTER 4

The United States Enters World War I

After the outbreak of World War I in 1914, the United States maintained its neutrality for almost three years. The policies of the German government, however, especially submarine warfare, angered President Wilson. Finally, in 1917, the United States entered World War I on the side of the Allies. Since the United States had never before become involved in a European war, Wilson's decision marked a major new direction in foreign policy.

Wilson's Second Term

In 1916, President Wilson ran for reelection on a platform that continued to favor neutrality. After the election, however, the United States began drifting closer to war. Early in 1917, the German government decided on a policy of unrestricted submarine warfare. This meant that German submarines would sink any ship approaching an English port. German leaders believed

▼ U.S. troops march near a training camp in Georgia during World War I.

that they had enough submarines to prevent Great Britain from receiving food or military supplies. As a result, Great Britain would be forced to drop out of the war and withdraw its support for France and Belgium.

Emperor William II realized that he risked a strong response from President Wilson. If Americans were killed on ships traveling to Britain, the United States might eventually be provoked into entering the war, giving the Allies the advantage against Germany. Germany was gambling that Great Britain would be forced to stop fighting before the United States could gather an army and send it to Europe.

Meanwhile, German diplomats were working on other plans to delay the United States' entrance into the war. German foreign minister Arthur Zimmerman sent a secret telegram to Mexico encouraging the Mexican government to become an ally of Germany and to invade southwestern United States. Such a move might enable Mexico to take back territory that it had lost to the United States during the Mexican-American War (1846–1848). When President Wilson received the telegram from the U.S. ambassador in Britain (who got it from the British Foreign Minister), he was outraged. The telegram was then published in American newspapers.

The Zimmerman telegram, combined with Germany's unrestricted submarine warfare, persuaded many Americans that war could no longer be avoided. Meanwhile, unrestricted warfare was taking a toll on U.S. ships taking supplies to England. On March 14, the U.S. ship *Algonquin* was sunk by a German U-boat near the coast of England. Four days later, three additional U.S. cargo ships were hit

▼ *The Zimmerman telegram, a coded 1917 message from German foreign minister Arthur Zimmerman to a Mexican official, offered to help Mexico regain territory it had lost to the United States in the Mexican-American War if Mexico would become an ally of Germany and invade the southwestern United States. The original telegram, which was intercepted and decoded by British naval officials, is part of the National Archives exhibit in Washington, D.C.*

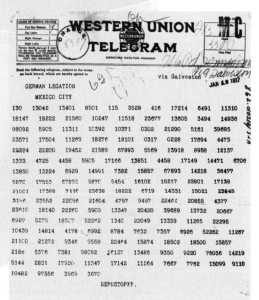

America in World War I

by the Germans, and four Americans were killed. On March 21, more Americans died on a tanker near the coast of Holland.

President Wilson decided that the United States must act to stop the deaths of Americans on neutral ships. On April 2, 1917, Wilson finally declared war on Germany. In a speech before Congress, Wilson said,

> It is a fearful thing to lead this great peaceful people into war, into the most terrible and disastrous of all wars, civilization itself seeming to be in the balance. But the right is more precious than peace, and we shall fight for the things which we have always carried nearest our hearts, for democracy.... To such a task we can dedicate our lives and our fortunes, everything that we are and everything that we have, with the pride of those who know that the day has come when America is privileged to spend her blood and her might for the principles that gave her birth and happiness and the peace which she has treasured.

▲ *A division of U.S.* ***destroyers*** *off the coast of Queenstown, Ireland, patrolled the North Atlantic shipping lanes between England and the United States, watching out for U-boats in order to ensure safe passage to Europe for supply ships.*

Wilson's War Aims

Wilson's aim was not only to defeat Germany and Austria-Hungary, which were ruled by **autocratic** emperors, but to "make the world safe for democracy." Wilson wanted to eliminate governments ruled by powerful kings and emperors. No leader before had stated such high ideals as a reason for going into war. President Wilson's principles about spreading democracy have influenced U.S. foreign policy ever since.

CHAPTER 5

The U.S. Army Goes to Europe

In 1917, the United States began building up an army to fight in Europe. Later in the year, the army, known as the American Expeditionary Force (AEF), started arriving in France.

The Draft

In 1917, when the United States entered World War I, there were only about 130,000 soldiers in its army. This force was far too small to oppose the German army, which had entered the war with more than two million men. Unlike in the Spanish-American War, President Wilson could not rely on volunteers to swell the size of the army enough to win a victory.

▼ President Woodrow Wilson (second from right in front row) leads a parade of drafted men in Washington, D.C., in 1917. He is accompanied by former president Theodore Roosevelt (third from right).

U.S. forces would still be too small. Therefore, the federal government began a **draft**. Congress passed a law that required young men to serve in the armed forces. There had not been a draft in the United States since the Civil War (1861–1865).

Training camps were established in towns across the United States. Draftees were trained by tough army sergeants who had very little time to turn U.S. youths into soldiers. A young soldier named Arthur Yensen wrote,

> I've been in the Army almost a month now. I have been bawled out [yelled at] for something every single day. I started in with fresh enthusiasm to do my bit; but instead of finding a history-book army full of noble heroes, all I've found is a pack of imps eternally giving me hell. I can stand the clothes, the drill is all right; but to have someone continually trying to take the joy out of life for no reason at all burns me up.

Going to Europe

Once their training was complete, the soldiers were loaded onto hundreds of trains that took them to the East Coast. There, they boarded troop ships in New York and other harbors and sailed for Europe. The Atlantic Ocean still contained German submarines waiting to torpedo American transport ships. Allied destroyers, however, had developed a new, more effective method of dealing with the threat. Instead of trying to find the submarines, the destroyers guarded the convoys of transports and waited for the Germans to come to them. When the enemy U-boats approached and began to launch torpedoes, they were attacked by groups of Allied destroyers that

AEF Training

When the U.S. troops arrived in France, they learned how to use **flamethrowers** and **tanks**, new weapons that had been introduced specifically for World War I. They were also taught how to use poison gas, which had first been used by the Germans in 1915 against the Allies on the Western Front. Both sides relied on poison gas, which was released before an attack and blown by the wind toward enemy defenders in the trenches. Gas was also fired at enemy trenches in artillery shells. To defend themselves against gas, U.S. soldiers were issued gas masks containing purified air. These masks protected soldiers against gases such as chlorine, which could kill anyone who inhaled it.

dropped explosives under the surface of the ocean. As a result, many German submarines were sunk, and most transport ships reached France safely.

The AEF

U.S. troops in France were part of the AEF under the command of John Pershing, the general who had led American forces into Mexico in pursuit of Pancho Villa. About 14,000 men arrived under General Pershing's command by June 1917. This number would swell to 200,000 by the end of the year.

Back home in the United States, building up a large army spurred the economy. Factories had to turn out thousands of uniforms, as well as vast quantities of ammunition, rifles, heavy artillery guns, naval ships, and other war supplies. The country rallied behind the war effort and industry surged.

The AEF in Europe

During 1917, the AEF arrived on the Western Front to find British and French troops exhausted by three years of war. Hundreds of thousands of Allied soldiers had already lost their lives assaulting the German defenses. French and British commanders wanted to move American troops into the front lines and give their own soldiers a rest. The U.S. forces would fill in for the Allied troops, who would be sent to the rear. General Pershing, however, resisted this suggestion. He wanted the AEF

▼ A French poster designed to create support for the war shows a soldier standing on a battlefield wearing a gas mask around his neck. Written in French behind the soldier, "On ne passe pas!" translates as "They shall not pass!" The phrase is believed to have originated with French general Robert Georges Nivelle at the Battle of Verdun in 1916 and refers here to keeping the Germans at bay during the Battle of the Marne.

America in World War I

to stay together as a unified fighting unit under his command. Pershing feared that U.S. troop units would be fed into battles, little by little, and killed off before they were fully ready to fight a major campaign. Then the AEF would not have the power to launch a strong enough attack to drive the Germans out of France.

Nevertheless, under pressure from the French and British, Pershing permitted some American troops to man the Allied trenches along the Western Front late in 1917. One soldier wrote,

> At several places along our trench there were narrow tunnels leading downward into the earth to our sleeping places. To enter, one had to stoop and descend into a dark, damp, smelly hole. When enough depth had been reached the tunnel widened and became level. Short cross tunnels led off of it. There one could sleep if he was tired enough. The whole place was infested with rats, body lice, and bed bugs.... I chose to stay in the firing trench [shooting at the enemy] in preference to that hole in the ground.

The German Offensive

By early 1918, a new crisis arose for the Allies along the Western Front. During the previous year, the brutal dictatorship of Nicholas II, the czar of Russia, was overthrown by the Russian army. A new government took power and called for democratic elections. A civil war broke out in Russia, pitting supporters of two different political ideologies, democracy and **communism**, against each other. Eventually, the communists took control of the government. Russia had been allied with France and England in World War I, but now the communists, led by V. I. Lenin, signed a

The Doughboys

The U.S. soldiers were known as "doughboys." Historians are not certain how this term arose. The American troops were better paid than the French soldiers. So the term *doughboy* may have referred to the extra dough (*dough* is a slang term for "money") that each soldier had in his pocket. The term *doughboy* also may have originated during the Spanish-American War. Soldiers fighting in the Philippines became covered with dust that mixed with their perspiration. The mixture sometimes looked like dough used for baking. *Doughboy* may also have arisen from the experiences of U.S. soldiers during the campaign against Pancho Villa. The soldiers lived in adobe (mud) huts, thus gaining the nickname "dobies."

Roosevelt's Sons in the War

Among the officers at Cantigny was Major Theodore Roosevelt, Jr., son of President Roosevelt. He led his troops in an attack that stopped a German advance and drove the enemy back from Cantigny. Lt. Quentin Roosevelt, another son of the former president, was a pilot during the war. In June 1918 he was killed when his plane was shot down by the Germans.

peace agreement with Germany and dropped out of the war. Germany then took most of its troops out of the **Eastern Front,** where they had been fighting against the Russians, and sent them to the Western Front in France and Belgium.

Along the Western Front, German soldiers outnumbered the French and British defenders. The German commanding generals, Paul von Hindenburg and Erich Ludendorff, decided to launch a series of attacks aimed at knocking the Allies out of the war. The German leaders realized that they had to defeat Britain and France before the U.S. troops were fully trained and ready to attack.

The German **offensive** began late in March 1918. British troops holding the northern sector of the Western Front suffered a stunning defeat at the hands of the Germans. Field Marshall Sir Douglas Haig, commander of the British forces, said that "their backs were to the wall." To prevent complete disaster, some AEF troops were rushed into the trenches to help the British defenders hold back the German advance. Meanwhile, thousands of additional U.S. troops arrived in Europe and headed for the front lines.

Ludendorff and Hindenburg continued to send their troops against the Allied defenses. In May, the AEF fought its first major battle of World War I. This was the battle of Cantigny in central France, where AEF forces attacked the German position. First, the AEF pounded the German trenches with heavy artillery. This bombardment was designed to kill many of the German soldiers and weaken their resistance. Captain Raymond Austin commanded some of the AEF artillery. "The ground was pounded to dust by our shells," he wrote. After this initial artillery attack, U.S. troops moved forward from the trenches across open fields while AEF artillery kept bombarding the Germans. The artillery shells fell just ahead of the troops as they advanced toward the German trenches. These shells killed more Germans, weakening their defenses against the attacking AEF. The U.S. **infantry** kept moving forward. "They walked steadily along behind our barrage [artillery attack] accompanied by the tanks which buzzed along with smoke coming out from their exhausts and their guns," Austin said. U.S. forces took Cantigny and held it against a furious German counterattack.

The German offensive continued in June as Germany concentrated its forces in the area east of Paris. German troops made a tremendous effort to capture the French capital. The German infantry advanced as far as Chateau-Thierry, a region only 40 miles (64 km) east of Paris. This area was part of the long Allied defense line. AEF troops advanced to a position alongside French forces holding the line. As Private William Francis recalled,

> The Germans came down the hill, firing everything at us, machine guns, rifle and hand grenades. We opened up immediately with our rifles and threw hand grenades as if they had been baseballs.... This lasted all through the night, and they finally decided that there was too many of us for them so they fell back to their old position.

By June 25, the AEF had captured an area called Belleau Wood. Although the casualties were very high, U.S. forces won an important victory, pushing back the Germans. Soon U.S. forces would begin an offensive to push the German army eastward out of France and back to Germany.

U.S. Air Power

During World War I, armies first began using airplanes. Planes were used to fly over enemy positions and bring back information that might help in an attack. Pilots also bombed trenches and fired on supply vehicles that were moving up to the front lines. Many Americans volunteered to become pilots during the war.

Among the best-known U.S. airmen was William (Billy) Mitchell. Mitchell had fought during the Spanish-American War and afterward served with the U.S. Army in the Philippines and Cuba. By the time the United States entered World War I, he had been named to lead the army's air division. Mitchell directed pilot training for the AEF in France. One of the men whom Mitchell trained was Captain Edward (Eddie) Rickenbacker. After his training, Rickenbacker became a member of the Ninety-Fourth Pursuit Squadron. Rickenbacker flew missions over France, shooting down German planes and strafing enemy positions. By September 1918, Rickenbacker was in charge of the squadron. He became known as the American Ace of Aces in World War I.

CHAPTER 6

The United States Is Victorious

The United States brought powerful military resources into World War I. Beginning in July 1918, the United States, along with the other Allies, defeated the last great German offensive of World War I. Then the Allies began pushing the weakened German army out of France. In November 1918, the war ended with Allied victory.

The Second Battle of the Marne

Allied forces had held back the Germans along the Western Front. In July 1918, the Allies and Germans clashed at the Second Battle of the Marne. The Germans made a last desperate effort to defeat the Allies and capture Paris. About 250,000 U.S. troops were arriving in France each month. As the Allied army grew more powerful, the Germans grew weaker.

The battle began with a huge artillery bombardment from the Germans. As they tried to cross the Marne River on boats, U.S. forces fired on them, sinking the boats. Allied artillery

▼ *This is a photo of U.S. troops from the Eighteenth Infantry, First Division, pausing in a ruined French town near St. Mihiel, France, in July 1918.*

then struck the German positions. "I will never forget the sight when our artillery opened up," recalled Private William Francis of the AEF. "It was worse than any electrical storm I have ever seen. The whole sky seemed to open up for it became as light as day." Along with French and British troops, the AEF attacked and drove back the Germans in some areas. The Germans successfully held on to other positions, however, and struggled to stop the advancing Allies.

In northern France, British troops pierced the German lines on August 8. General Ludendorff called it "the Black Day in the history of the German Army in the war." Gradually, the added strength of AEF forces became too much for the Germans, and they began to retreat. By mid-August, the Second Battle of the Marne was over, and the Allies had won a convincing victory.

U.S. Troops in the Allied Offensive

After mid-August, German troops found themselves completely on the defensive. In September 1918, the AEF attacked the German position at St. Mihiel, southeast of Paris. The attack started with a heavy artillery barrage. Then the AEF advanced toward the German lines. Upon reaching the enemy trenches, the U.S. doughboys found that many of the German soldiers had already retreated. Although the enemy later tried to retake the St. Mihiel position, the AEF drove back the attacks.

Meuse-Argonne Offensive

In September, U.S. troops joined a huge Allied push along the Meuse River and the Argonne Forest in France. This offensive was aimed at driving the Germans back 30 miles (48 km) into eastern France.

Sergeant York

One of the soldiers involved in the Meuse-Argonne offensive was Corporal Alvin York, a member of the Eighty-second Infantry Division.

On October 8, York and his fellow soldiers prepared to charge a German machine gun position. Before the attack, they were hit by a heavy artillery barrage and shells containing gas. The U.S. soldiers strapped on their gas masks and began to charge, although many were killed. "Our boys just went down like the long grass before the mowing machine at home," York wrote in his diary. The U.S. troops fell back and seventeen of them began to move around the German flank, capturing several of the enemy. The German machine gunners, realizing they had been outflanked, turned around and began firing at York and the other soldiers. York took up a position behind a tree and began picking off the Germans. "I don't think I missed a shot," he wrote. "It was no time to miss." York captured 132 prisoners and was awarded the **Congressional Medal of Honor**.

The offensive included 1.2 million doughboys from the AEF. Accompanying the infantry troops were about 190 tanks and 600 planes flown by U.S. pilots. German forces put up a strong defense along the hills, which were crisscrossed with miles of trenches and barbed wire. The offensive began in late September and continued until early November.

The German armies put up a stubborn defense, and the AEF suffered heavy casualties. Meanwhile, weather conditions grew worse as rains increased during the fall. The wheels of the heavy artillery bogged down in muddy roadways that were flooded from the rainfall.

The offensive stalled and the German lines held. In early October, the AEF launched another attack. The doughboys advanced slowly and took heavy casualties—seventy-five thousand by mid-October.

Negotiations for Peace

Meanwhile, German leaders had begun negotiations with the Allies to end the war. Germany realized that it could not achieve victory. The Allies had not only more soldiers, but more supplies, including a far greater number of tanks, artillery, and airplanes.

America in World War I

Most important, the number of soldiers in the AEF was growing weekly as more and more U.S. troops arrived in France.

Negotiations between Germany and the Allies went on during October. Meanwhile the fighting continued, and the AEF launched its largest attack on November 1, 1918. As Private Malcolm Aitken of the AEF recalled,

> From November 1st until 9th it was one continuous scrap. We would clean up one [enemy] nest [hideout] and then find another twice as bad. Woods and brush and individual spots hid these machine guns and they were very difficult to dislodge. You see there was so much crossfire from the riflemen and other machine guns, that you didn't know which one to get first.

Germany could not withstand the continuing Allied assaults. On November 11, 1918, the German generals met the Allied commanders inside a railroad car at Compiègne, France, and signed an **armistice** agreement, ending the war. Suddenly, the guns on the Western Front fell silent.

The news reached the United States early on the morning of November 11. Celebrations broke out in many towns, as people poured into the streets, hugging and kissing each other. They honked their car horns and marched in large parades. The war, however, had taken a terrible toll in casualties. The AEF, which totaled 1.3 million men on the Western Front, had more than 50,000 troops killed and more than 200,000 wounded. British casualties numbered more than 900,000. The French lost 1.7 million dead, and 2 million Germans were killed. World War I had destroyed an entire generation of young men throughout the world.

Fast Fact

Germany's defeat at the Second Battle of the Marne led many German commanders to believe the war was lost. It became the last major attempt by the Central Powers to win World War I.

CHAPTER 7

Aftermath of War

W orld War I was called the "war to end all wars." President Woodrow Wilson hoped that his plans for peace would prevent any similar war from breaking out again.

The Fourteen Points

When it became likely that the United States would join the Allies fighting in World War I, President Wilson formulated a program called the Fourteen Points. He hoped that it would be the basis of an eventual peace agreement. For example, the program called for guaranteeing freedom of the seas for every nation and reducing the number of military arms that each nation possessed in order to help prevent a future world war. Point Fourteen contained Wilson's vision of a **League of Nations,** a world body where disputes might be settled without war and which would protect each nation from invasion by its neighbors. President Wilson's war aims guided the United States as it entered World War I. Wilson, along with many other Americans, hoped

▼ *U.S. president Woodrow Wilson announces the end of World War I and reads the terms of the armistice to Congress on November 11, 1918. The terms of the armistice and the peace plan proposals are outlined in Wilson's Fourteen Points.*

that the United States would not only help the Allies win the war but prevent another world war from ever breaking out again.

The Treaty of Versailles

In December 1918, after the armistice, President Wilson journeyed to France to draft a peace treaty that would bring a formal end to World War I. Europeans hailed Wilson's arrival, grateful for the role played by the United States in winning World War I. Wilson was joined by David Lloyd George, the prime minister of Great Britain; Georges Clemenceau, the prime minister of France; and Vittorio Orlando, the prime minister of Italy. Only the Allies participated in the discussions. The German and Austro-Hungarian leaders were not permitted to attend the peace conference.

Wilson wanted to create a peace treaty based on his Fourteen Points. No peace conference had ever before come together to discuss such a set of idealistic principles. President Wilson believed in the Fourteen Points, but British and French leaders did not want a "peace without victory." Britain, France, and Italy insisted on imposing a very harsh peace agreement on Germany. Germany was held responsible for causing the war and forced to pay $15 billion to the Allies. Germany lost the territory it had taken from France in the Franco-Prussian War (1870–1871). The Austro-Hungarian Empire was broken up into independent countries, each with a single nationality.

▲ This 1920 political cartoon indicates that Henry Cabot Lodge was to blame for the Senate's failure to approve U.S. membership in the League of Nations. The animal skin in the cartoon, representing the League of Nations, hangs on the door of "Cabot Lodge," implying that Senator Lodge "killed" the bill.

President Wilson accepted these terms because the Treaty of Versailles called for the establishment of the League of Nations. To the president, creating the League of Nations to preserve peace in the world was the most important element of his peace proposal. The Allies agreed to join the League of Nations only if Wilson accepted the other terms of the treaty.

After signing the Treaty of Versailles in June 1919, President Wilson returned to the United States. According to the U.S. Constitution, the Senate had to approve any treaty signed by the president. The Senate, however, was controlled by Republicans. Wilson had not asked any of them to accompany him to Versailles and participate in the peace discussions. This insult irritated powerful Republican leaders, such as Senator Henry Cabot Lodge, who, in turn, opposed the League of Nations and the Treaty of Versailles.

President Wilson tried to gather support for the League of Nations. Many Americans, however, had grown tired of Europe and its problems. They wanted a return to the policies of the past, before World War I, when the United States had stayed out of European affairs. U.S. membership in the League of Nations was never approved by the U.S. Senate. The United States began once again to reduce its role in world affairs.

The United States in the 1920s

In 1920, voters elected Republican Warren Harding president of the United States. Unlike President Wilson, Harding opposed the League of Nations and wanted the nation to play a smaller role in world affairs. The United States, which had helped win World War I, could not suddenly abandon the world stage. Therefore, during the 1920s, Republican

America in World War I

diplomats participated in several international conferences. In 1921, the Washington Armament Conference included representatives from the United States, France, Italy, and Japan. These nations agreed not to build large armed warships for a decade. In 1928, the United States and fifteen other nations signed the Pact of Paris. This agreement called on nations to solve their differences by peaceful negotiations instead of going to war.

While the United States remained involved in world affairs, its major focus was inward. Most people wanted to forget about the brutality and bloodshed of war. During the 1920s, the United States experienced an economic boom. As Calvin Coolidge, who was president from 1923 to 1929 said, the "business of America is business." Cities grew larger as more and more tall buildings, called skyscrapers, were built. Consumers spent money on new items, such as refrigerators and automobiles. In fact, the number of automobiles grew by 27 million during the 1920s. The 1920s were known as the Jazz Age, as Americans went to nightclubs and danced to jazz bands.

Radical changes, however, were occurring in Europe. By the 1930s, a new threat had arisen in Germany. German dictator Adolf Hitler urged his people to tear up the Treaty of Versailles, rebuild their armies, and take back the territories that they had lost. U.S. leaders, afraid of returning to international conflict and without public support at home, did little or nothing to oppose Hitler. This complacency would not last long, however. In 1939, Germany began a new world war that was far more devastating than the first one. The United States would have no choice, in the end, but to become involved. World War II would make the United States a major global power, a position it would never retreat from again.

Fast Fact

Between 1920 and 1929, manufacturing in the United States grew more than 60 percent.

TIME LINE

1823	The Monroe Doctrine is issued by President James Monroe.
1893	Lorrin Thurston leads overthrow of the Hawaiian government.
1896	Republican William McKinley is elected president.
1898	The United States annexes Hawaii and wins the Spanish-American War.
1901	President McKinley is assassinated; Theodore Roosevelt becomes president.
1903	Roosevelt supports revolt in Panama; the United States signs a treaty with Panama to build a canal across its territory.
1904	Roosevelt issues the Corollary to the Monroe Doctrine.
1905	U.S. government takes control of the finances of the Dominican Republic.
1907	Roosevelt sends the Great White Fleet around the world.
1908	William Howard Taft is elected president.
1912	Woodrow Wilson is elected president.
1913	The Plattsburg Movement begins to train U.S. military officers.
1914	The United States invades Mexico; World War I begins; German armies invade Belgium and France.
1915	A German submarine sinks the *Lusitania*.
1916	A German submarine sinks the *Sussex*; General Pershing leads U.S. troops into Mexico; Allies fight Germans at Battle of Verdun and Battle of Somme; Wilson is reelected.
1917	Germany begins a policy of unrestricted submarine warfare; the Zimmerman telegram helps provoke the United States into war; the United States enters World War I on the side of the Allies.
1918	President Wilson announces the Fourteen Points; Russia drops out of World War I; U.S. troops participate in major battles; Allies win Second Battle of the Marne; German armies sign armistice agreement; World War I ends.
1919	The Treaty of Versailles is signed in France; the U.S. Senate votes against joining the League of Nations.
1920	Warren Harding is elected president.
1921	The Washington Armament Conference restricts levels of naval forces.
1928	The United States and other nations sign the Pact of Paris, aimed at avoiding war.
1933	Adolf Hitler becomes chancellor of Germany.
1939	Germany begins World War II.

GLOSSARY

annex to make part of a larger country

armistice a temporary end to military conflict

artillery heavy guns, such as cannons

autocratic ruling with unlimited authority, like a dictator or king

barbed wire steel wire with sharp metal points at regular intervals

battleships large, heavily armored warships with many guns

blockade to prevent supplies from moving into an enemy nation

canal a waterway built to improve transportation or navigation

communism system of government in which the state plans and controls the economy and a single, authoritarian party holds power, claiming to make progress toward a society in which all goods are equally shared by the people

Congressional Medal of Honor the highest award given to an American soldier for bravery in battle

cruisers large, heavily armored warships that are smaller than battleships

democracy government by the voters and their representatives

destroyers large warships with metal armor and big artillery

Dollar Diplomacy foreign policy pursued by President William H. Taft that encouraged investors to put their money into Latin America to increase U.S. influence over the region

draft an order for individuals to enter the armed forces

Eastern Front battleground between Russia and Germany in Eastern Europe

flamethrowers weapons for shooting fire at an enemy

flanking movement an effort by an army to move around its enemy and attack it from the rear

fortify to build defenses to safeguard a military position

hacienda a large estate

infantry soldiers who fight on foot

League of Nations the world body established in 1919 to prevent war and encourage negotiations to solve differences between nations

Monroe Doctrine President Monroe's 1823 doctrine that the United States opposed any attempt by European nations to establish colonies in the Western hemisphere

negotiations efforts to reach an agreement between two sides in conflict

neutral describing a nation that does not join any side in a war

offensive a large, coordinated attack by many troops

stalemate an evenly matched contest between two opposing sides

tanks armored vehicles with heavy artillery

torpedoes explosive shells fired by a submarine

Western Front trenches that ran 475 miles (760 km) from Belgian coast to Switzerland during World War I

Books

Golay, Michael. *Spanish-American War.* Facts On File, 2003.

Hamilton, John. *Aircraft of World War I.* Abdo & Daughters Publishing, 2003.

Lewis, Jon E., editor. *The Mammoth Book of Eyewitness World War I.* Carroll & Graf, 2004.

Smolinski, Diane. *Soldiers of the Spanish-American War.* Heinemann Library, 2003.

Willmott, H. P. *World War I.* Dorling Kindersley, 2006.

Worth, Richard. *Gunpowder.* Chelsea House, 2004.

Web Sites

Roosevelt, Theodore. *The Rough Riders.* *www.bartleby.com/51/4.html*

The World War I Document Archive. *www.lib.byu.edu/~rdh/wwi/*

York, Alvin. *The Diary of Alvin York.* *acacia.pair.com/Acacia.Vignettes/The.Diary.of.Alvin.York.html*

INDEX

About the Author

Richard Worth is the author of more than fifty nonfiction books for young adults. These include biographies, history, and current events, as well as a series on the criminal justice system. In 2004, his book *Gangs and Crime* was named one of the Best Books for the Teenage List by the New York Public Library. Worth also runs training programs in business writing and public speaking for Fortune 100 companies in the United States and Europe. In addition, he has been a volunteer teacher of writing to third graders in the Bridgeport, Connecticut, public school system for the past decade.